Sacramento, CA 95814
06/18

THIS BOOK WAS DONATED BY
The Sacramento Public Library Foundation
Books and Materials Endowment

The Sacramento Public Library gratefully acknowledges this contribution to support and improve Library services in the community.

SACRAMENTO PUBLIC LIBRARY

Savvy

MAKEUP & SKIN HACKS
YOUR SKIN SITUATIONS SOLVED!

BY REBECCA RISSMAN

CAPSTONE PRESS
a capstone imprint

Savvy Books are published by Capstone Press,
1710 Roe Crest Drive, North Mankato,
Minnesota 56003
www.mycapstone.com

Copyright © 2018 by Capstone Press, a Capstone imprint. All rights reserved. No part of this publication may be reproduced in whole or in part, or stored in a retrieval system, or transmitted in any form or by any means, electronic, mechanical, photocopying, recording, or otherwise, without written permission of the publisher.

Library of Congress Cataloging-in-Publication Data
Names: Rissman, Rebecca, author.
Title: Makeup and skin hacks : your skin situations solved! / by Rebecca Rissman.
Description: North Mankato, Minnesota : Capstone Press, [2017] | Series: Beauty hacks | Audience: Age 14. | Audience: Grade 7 to 8. | Includes bibliographical references.
Identifiers: LCCN 2017004400 (print) | LCCN 2017009211 (ebook) | ISBN 9781515768289 (library binding) | ISBN 9781515768326 (eBook PDF)
Subjects: LCSH: Skin—Care and hygiene—Juvenile literature.
Classification: LCC RL87 .R57 2017 (print) | LCC RL87 (ebook) | DDC 646.7/26—dc23
LC record available at https://lccn.loc.gov/2017004400

Editorial Credits
Mandy Robbins, editor; Aruna Rangarajan, designer; Kelli Lageson and Morgan Walters, media researchers; Kathy McColley, production specialist

Photo Credits
All photos by Capstone Studio: Karon Dubke, except: Amy Mokris, 48, inset; Capstone Press: Aruna Rangarajan, 26 (middle), 33 (top); Shutterstock: Africa Studio, cover (back cover makeup items), 14 (top right), 28 (top), aimy27feb, 21 (top), AMS Studio, 23, AnastasiiaM, 32 (bottom), Anastasiya Domnitch, 37 (top), Ann Haritonenko, 2, 31 (top), Ariwasabi, 4, artproem, 17 (left), Asia Images Group, 33 (bottom), aslysun, 42, AYakovlev, 18 (top right), Claudia K, 32 (top), Damir Khabirov, 31 (bottom right), Djomas, 20, 24, Dmitry A, 26 (back), enchanted_fairy, 29 (bottom middle), Fotoluminate LLC, 29 (top), Freedom_Studio, 39 (top right), givaga, 15 (middle right), Halay Alex, 34, Jacob Lund, 6 (bottom), JAYANNPO, 21 (bottom), jocic, 39 (cotton ball), Kaponia Aliaksei, 28 (bottom), kireewong foto, 6 (top), Kucher Serhii, 25 (marker), manzrussali, cover, mimagephotography, 46, miya227, 14 (bottom), Nikkolia, 10, novazelandia, 37 (middle left), 37 (bottom left), 37 (right), Odua Images, 30, Oksana Shufrych, 7, OmniArt, 39 (makeup), paffy, 38, photastic, 47 (index card), popcorner, 36 (back), Robyn Mackenzie, 25 (tape), RomarioIen, 12, ronstik, 29 (bottom left), Stephanie Zieber, 17 (right), studioloco, 19 (back), SunKids, 44, Sviridov Vitaly, 39 (cotton swab), Svitlana Sokolova, 8 (back), urfin, cover (back cover top right)

Design elements: Shutterstock

Printed and bound in the USA.
010373F17

TABLE OF CONTENTS

INTRODUCTION
Skin Wins And Helpful Hacks 4

CHAPTER 1
Acne Hacks 12

CHAPTER 2
Fragrance Hacks 16

CHAPTER 3
Makeup Tips And Tricks 20

CHAPTER 4
Prepping Your Canvas 24

CHAPTER 5
Eye-Catching Eyes 30

CHAPTER 6
Lip Hacks To Love 34

CHAPTER 7
Keep It Clean   40

CHAPTER 8
Your On-The-Go Essentials 44

CHAPTER 9
Be Your Best Self   46

Read More 48

About The Author 48

INTRODUCTION
SKIN WINS AND HELPFUL HACKS

Beauty Hacks are SIMPLE TRICKS that EVERYONE CAN DO

They can turn cosmetic catastrophes into makeup masterpieces. They can transform acne agony into super-smooth skin. And they bring out your inner innovator at the same time.

The best skincare is often the simplest. This book will teach you quick, easy, and gentle ways to take care of your skin and bring out your inner beauty.

Lots of people wear makeup to enhance their inner and outer beauty. Makeup can be a great way to express yourself and feel more confident. It can be simple and subdued or it can be wild. One of the best things about makeup is that it's not permanent.

SUPPLIES NEEDED

* sea salt
* lemons
* spray bottle
* resealable jars
* olive oil
* tea tree oil
* unscented lotion
* baby shampoo
* saline solution
* microplane

HELPFUL TIPS FOR YOU

Tip #1 You can find tea tree oil at your local drugstore, or ask a parent to buy it for you online.

Tip #2 Remember to do a skin test for any new product before using it on your face. Just dab a tiny bit on the skin of your inner elbow. Then wait about two days. If your skin gets red, itchy, or painful, do not use the product.

Tip #3 Be extra careful using products around your eyes. This skin is very sensitive, as are your eyes themselves.

Tip #4 The secret to glowing, healthy skin isn't some expensive department store product. It's water. More than half of your body is made up of water. Most doctors recommend drinking at least eight glasses of it per day.

Save Your Skin WITH SALT

Is dull skin getting you down? Had enough of rough patches? There's a simple beauty hack to soothe your skin. And the ingredients are right in your kitchen.

Salt is a great exfoliator. It can be used to gently rub away dead skin cells. This allows newer, healthier skin to shine. When mixed with a moisturizing ingredient, such as oil, salt can quickly and gently rejuvenate your skin.

HOMEMADE BODY SCRUB:

WHAT YOU NEED:

- ½ cup sea salt
- ½ cup olive oil
- 1 lemon
- fine cheese grater or microplane
- bowl and spoon
- resealable jar

WHAT TO DO:

Step 1 Combine oil and salt in a bowl. Stir well.

Step 2 Use the grater or microplane to scrape the peel of about half the lemon. Collect the zest, and add it to the oil and salt mixture. Stir well.

Step 3 Transfer salt scrub to reusable jar.

Step 4 Use the scrub while in a warm shower. Take a small amount of the salt scrub into your palm or onto a washcloth. Rub it onto your skin in gentle, circular motions. Rinse well.

SPICE IT UP

Mix up your homemade beauty concoctions by adding some of your favorite herbs or spices.

LAVENDER
Dried lavender or rosemary gives your scrub a relaxing scent.

GROUND CARDAMOM SEEDS
Cardamom can give your scrub a bold, yet relaxing, scent.

CINNAMON
Cinnamon or espresso can turn your scrub into an invigorating wake-up call.

TURMERIC
Turmeric adds healing properties to your scrub and relaxes sore muscles.

ORANGE PEEL
Orange peel could transform your scrub into an invigorating experience to wake you up in the morning.

PUMPKIN SPICE
Adding a bit of pumpkin spice could put you in an autumn mood.

YOUR OWN SEASIDE SPRITZ

Have you ever noticed that your skin seems to glow after a day at the beach? It isn't just from the sunshine. The salt found in seawater helps clear away blemishes for some people.

The good news is, you can capture that beach-perfect skin without taking a trip to the seaside. A quick trip to your pantry is the only travel you'll need to do.

WHAT YOU NEED:

1 tablespoon sea salt + 16 ounces warm water + 1 spray bottle + 1 washcloth

WHAT TO DO:

Step 1 Fill the spray bottle with 16 ounces of warm water.

Step 2 Add 1 tablespoon of sea salt to the water. Shake well.

Step 3 Hold the bottle at arm's length. Close your eyes, and spray it directly onto your clean face. Let it air dry, and wipe off any excess.

Sea Salt Vs. Table Salt

Most beauty hacks involving salt recommend using **sea salt** instead of **table salt**. Ever wondered why? Here's an easy way to compare the two:

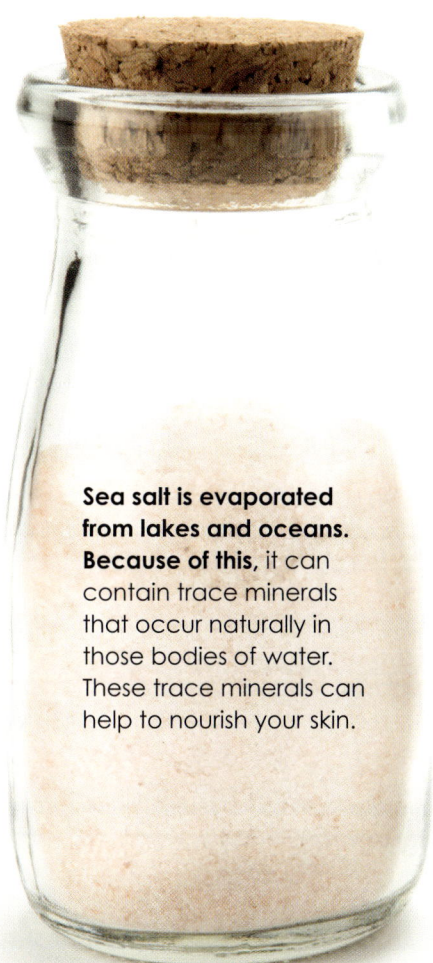

Sea salt is evaporated from lakes and oceans. Because of this, it can contain trace minerals that occur naturally in those bodies of water. These trace minerals can help to nourish your skin.

The chemicals used to process table salt make it harsher on skin. If you have sensitive skin, stick to the sea salt. If your skin isn't sensitive, you could substitute table salt for a foot or body scrub, but don't use it on the delicate skin of your face.

SUMMER SKIN HACKS

Suntanned skin has a beautiful golden glow, but it also comes with the risk of skin cancer and premature wrinkles. Make sure that you're safe in the sun with these summer skin tips:

- ▶ Use a sunscreen with a sun protection factor (**SPF) of 30** or higher.

- ▶ Apply sunscreen to **any exposed skin** — face, neck, hands, arms, legs, and even feet.

- ▶ Apply sunscreen at least **15 minutes** before you go outside.

- ▶ Re-apply sunscreen **every two hours.** If you've been swimming or sweating a lot, reapply even sooner.

WHIP UP SOME BRONZER

Get the glow you want and keep your skin safe using bronzer. This recipe for homemade bronzer is fast, easy, and smells amazing. You'll have the warm glow you want in no time!

WHAT YOU NEED:

1 teaspoon cinnamon + 1 teaspoon nutmeg  + 1 teaspoon unsweetened cocoa powder + 1 teaspoon cornstarch

1 tablespoon avocado oil  + empty makeup compact  + fork, spoon, and bowl

WHAT TO DO:

Step 1 Wash and dry your hands. Clean fingers are essential when you're dealing with anything that will touch your face.

Step 2 Add cinnamon, nutmeg, cocoa powder, and cornstarch into the bowl, and mix well with the fork.

Step 3 Adjust the color to match your skin tone by adding more cocoa, nutmeg, or cornstarch.

Step 4 Add a few drops of avocado oil and mix well. The oil will help you press the bronzer down into the compact.

Step 5 Carefully spoon bronzer powder into compact, and press it down. If the mixture is too crumbly to stay in the compact, return it to the bowl and add more oil. Then try putting it into the compact again.

> **Tip**
> Store your homemade bronzer in a cool, dark place, such as your medicine cabinet. It should last a few months and get you through the summer season.

Over the years, hundreds of tips and tricks have been used to help zap zits. Some of these treatments are simple and effective. Others are a little more extreme. Some are even dangerous. But one of the best ways to arm yourself against zits is to learn what not to do. Here are a few common treatments that dermatologists advise against.

CHAPTER 1
ACNE HACKS

▶ LEMON AND LIME JUICE

Do not rub lemon juice on your face — especially if you plan on going outside. The acid in the juice can cause a streaky brown rash on sun-kissed skin.

▶ PICKING, POPPING, PRODDING, POKING

Got a zit? Leave it be. The worst thing you can do is aggravate it by picking and popping. Picking at acne can introduce bacteria, and bacteria can cause infections. Popping can also lead to permanent acne scars.

▶ TOOTHPASTE

Have you ever heard that toothpaste is a great zit remedy? Well, it used to be. The basic ingredients in simple toothpastes can actually help dry out a blemish. These include baking soda, hydrogen peroxide, alcohol, and some essential oils. However, most modern toothpastes include additional ingredients. Whiteners, tartar fighters, and strong scents can actually make the condition of your skin worse.

BLAST BLEMISHES WITH TEA TREE OIL

Even with a regular cleansing routine, pimples can still pop up. What should you do to ban blemishes that appear out of nowhere? **Try tea tree oil.** This type of oil can open up your pores. It also has disinfecting properties to clean out any grime in there.

WHAT YOU NEED:

 tea tree oil

\+

 gentle facial cleanser

Tip: If you have sensitive skin, dilute the tea tree oil with a few drops of vitamin E oil or olive oil.

WHAT TO DO:

Wash your face with a gentle cleanser, and pat skin dry. Soak the end of a cotton swab with two drops of tea tree oil. Gently dab cotton swab directly onto the blemish, and let your skin air dry.

There are many causes for acne. Oil, clogged pores, and bacteria are some of the most common. Hormonal changes, such as puberty, can also lead to breakouts. The best way to prevent acne is to simply wash your face with a gentle cleanser twice a day. Gentle cleansers are soaps that do not include harsh ingredients, fragrances, or chemicals. If you have especially sensitive skin, you might want to try baby wash.

ICE IT!

One unfortunate side effect of acne can be that it makes your skin red and swollen. You can reduce redness and swelling by icing blemishes down.

WHAT YOU NEED:

1 thin washcloth

+

1 ice cube

+

gentle facial cleanser

WHAT TO DO:

Step 1 Wash your face with a gentle cleanser, and pat skin dry.

Step 2 Wrap the ice cube in a thin washcloth. Hold the wrapped ice cube against your blemish for 1 minute. Wait 5 minutes. Repeat with a fresh ice cube if desired.

Fact: If gently cleansing your face two times a day for at least six weeks doesn't improve your pimple situation, it might be time to visit a dermatologist. This skin doctor can prescribe a stronger type of facial cleanser.

CHAPTER 2
FRAGRANCE HACKS

Are you obsessed with scents? Do you consider yourself a perfume perfectionist? If you love getting the most out of your fragrances, you'll want to be sure you know these hacks.

DAB, DON'T RUB

A lot of people dab perfume on their wrists, which works just fine. But don't rub them together. When you do this, you change the way your perfume smells. Rubbing also ensures that your perfume won't last very long.

HEAVENLY HAIR

If your hair smells oily, spray your hairbrush with perfume before running it through your locks. It will lightly scent your hair. Spraying perfume directly onto your hair is a bad idea. It will cause your hair to feel dry and brittle.

MAKE YOUR OWN SCENTED LOTION

Have you ever used a favorite perfume until all that remains are a few drops? Instead of tossing the bottle, make your own scented lotion and enjoy your beloved scent a little longer. Just mix ½ – 1 cup of unscented lotion with the remaining drops of perfume. Store your new concoction in a resealable container and enjoy.

MAKE YOUR SCENT LAST

To give your perfume extra staying power, spray it onto moisturized skin. You can do this a few different ways.

1. Spray your perfume on right after you've toweled off from your shower.

2. Use unscented body lotion before spraying your perfume.

3. Apply a thin layer of Vaseline before spraying perfume.

Apply Perfume HERE

- inner wrists
- inner elbows
- back of ear
- base of neck
- back of knees

For a light scent all over, give your perfume a pump in front of you and walk through the mist.

→ Give Stinky Feet
THE BOOT

There's nothing more distracting than a foul odor. Bathing regularly is obviously a must, but sometimes awkward odors still creep up. Whether it's coming from your old running shoes or your armpits, smelling bad stinks. And you don't want to just cover it up with fragrances. Try these hacks to be sure you always smell fresh.

WHAT YOU NEED:

- bowl of warm water big enough to fit both feet
- 2 tablespoons baking soda
- 1 lemon
- dry towel

WHAT TO DO:

Fill a bowl with warm (but not hot) water. Stir in baking soda and the juice of one lemon. Soak your feet in the water for 15 – 20 minutes. Use a clean towel to thoroughly dry your feet.

FIX STINKY PITS

Fight foul odors while you sleep. Try this hack before you go to bed at night to help fight armpit odor.

WHAT YOU NEED:

tea tree oil

+

 1 cup water

+

spray bottle

WHAT TO DO:

Thoroughly wash and dry your armpits. Pour water into the spray bottle, and add two drops of tea tree oil. Shake well. Spray onto armpits and allow to air dry.

Have you ever looked in your cosmetics bag and realized you've forgotten half your essentials? All right, take a deep breath. A little makeup mishap is nothing you can't handle.

CHAPTER 3
MAKEUP TIPS AND TRICKS

CHEEK TRICKS

If you're out on the town and discover you're out of blush, try this quick fix. Dab a little lipstick or lip gloss on your cheeks and rub it in. Matte colors add a deep pop of color. Cream products add moisture to your rosy cheeks.

LIGHT UP A ROOM

Do you want to enhance your natural glow? Dab a bit of shimmer on key areas. Try tapping some just under your outer eyebrows. Add a little to the top of your cheekbones. Use a clean finger or cotton swab to dab some right next to your tear ducts. You'll be amazed at the difference this trick can make.

SHINY SITUATION

Oil blotting sheets do a great job of quickly absorbing the shine on your nose, forehead, cheeks, and chin. But what happens when you're out on the town and fresh out of blotting sheets? Before you think about heading to the drugstore, check the closest public restroom. If you see paper toilet seat covers, you're in luck. They are made of the same material as your tiny blotting papers. But they're much bigger. Tear a clean toilet seat cover into small squares and use them to blot away excess oil. Fold up a few extra pieces and tuck them in your purse or backpack to prepare for touchups.

BLUSHING BEAUTY

If blush is the only makeup product you have on hand, use it to bring out your natural glow. Dab a bit on your eyelids for a fresh and healthy look. Use it on your cheeks as usual. And rub some onto your lips for a light lip stain.

If you have lip balm or lip gloss available, put it on your lips first before you dab on the blush. Using blush as a lipstick provides a more matte coverage than the typical lipstick. That means it lasts longer too. But don't make a habit of using blush on your lips, as it can dry them out.

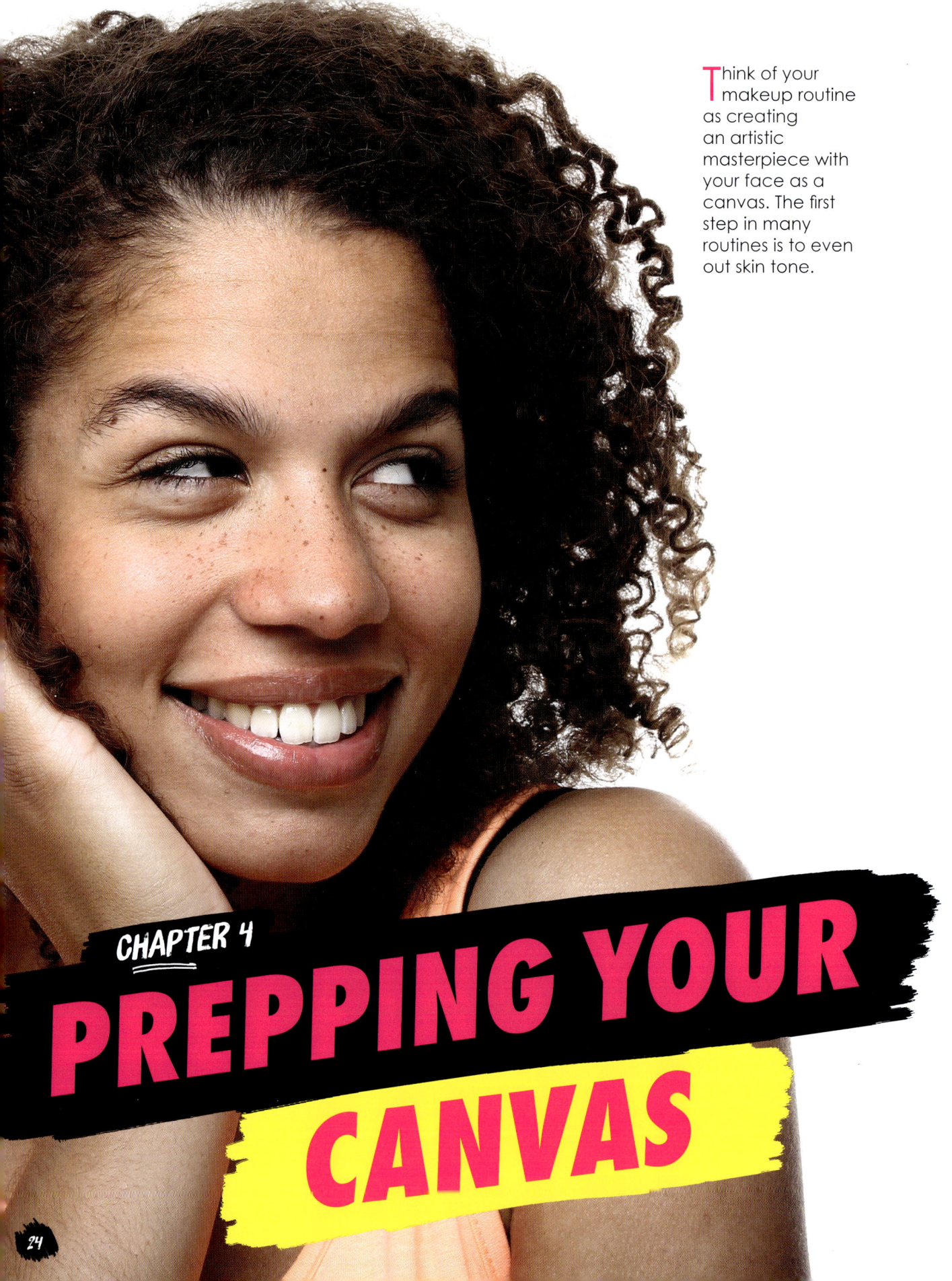

Think of your makeup routine as creating an artistic masterpiece with your face as a canvas. The first step in many routines is to even out skin tone.

CHAPTER 4
PREPPING YOUR CANVAS

Foundation is often a girl's go-to for prepping her face. It can be liquid or powder, and a little goes a long way. Thick foundation can look cakey and clog your pores. If you use it at all, use a thin layer. Concealer is a makeup tool that helps cover blemishes, under-eye circles, and many other imperfections. It is usually a thick liquid or paste. Foundation and concealer should not entirely cover up your gorgeous skin. If you're wearing them the right way, they wil highlight it.

MAKE YOUR OWN TINTED MOISTURIZER

Sometimes, you might want less coverage on your face than what foundation and concealers provide. Tinted moisturizers are great for the natural look. They often combine moisturizer, sunscreen, and a small amount of color. If you're all out of tinted moisturizer, it's easy to make your own.

WHAT YOU NEED:

bowl and spoon	liquid foundation	unscented lotion	marker	masking tape or label	resealable jar

WHAT TO DO:

Put a few spoonfuls of unscented lotion into the bowl. Mix in one spoonful of foundation. Add more foundation or lotion to get the coverage you desire. Transfer the mixture to the resealable jar. Label the jar so you remember what is inside. It's good for up to two years!

CREATIVE CONCEALER

Try using concealer creatively. Here are a few ways it can boost your beauty:

Concealer is an especially handy item to keep in your makeup bag. It is thicker than foundation, so it provides more coverage. It's also often a little tacky or sticky. This gives it staying power. Dust it with a little face power, and you'll be set for the day.

POWER PRIMER

Apply a thin coat of concealer to your eyelids before you apply your eye shadow. The sticky concealer will work as a primer and help your eye shadow last all day.

BROW POWER

Dab a little concealer under the arch of your eyebrows for a natural-looking highlight.

LIP LINER

Try applying a small amount of concealer around your lips before applying a bright or dark lipstick. Doing this will help keep your lip color from spreading and smearing. You can also apply it on your lips to give lipstick more staying power.

APPLICATION OPTIONS

You can use different tools for applying concealer. Some concealers come with their own application wand. You can also use beauty sponges, a medium-width brush, or your clean middle finger. The pad of your middle finger is wider and softer than your pointer.

RIGHT VS. WRONG

Most people apply concealer under their eyes the wrong way. Instead of applying it in half moons under your eyes, you should apply it in deep triangles that point down. Doing it this way brightens up your face. It makes you look fresh-faced and energetic.

FIND THE RIGHT HUE

Foundations come in a rainbow of shades. The best way to find the right one for your skin tone is to try it. Dip a cotton swab into the color and apply the makeup down your jawline. If it's hard to see, then you've found the right color! Your concealer should be one or two shades lighter than your foundation. If you don't want to test out cosmetics on your face, try putting a little on your chest.

Foundation Fix

If you need the coverage of a concealer but you don't have any, use your foundation to make your own. Use your fingertip to dab a small drop of liquid foundation on your blemish. Wait three to five minutes to allow the foundation to begin to dry. When it becomes tacky, use your finger to gently pat the spot until it blends.

COLOR CORRECTION

Have you ever tried lavender or mint green concealer? What about orange? If these colors have you thinking about art class more than your makeup bag, think again. Check out this chart to learn how to use colors to even out your skin.

ORANGE: cancels out dark spots on dark skin tones

YELLOW: conceals dark shadows on olive or tan skin tones

GREEN: conceals redness on most skin tones

LAVENDER: cancels out yellow spots on most skin tones

PINK: evens out dark circles and blue tints in pale skin

PEACH: covers dark circles and shadows on medium skin

LOOK FRESH FAST

If you don't have much time before dashing out the door, you only need three items for a fresh face fast.

1. Dab a little concealer onto any blemishes and dark circles.

2. Swipe a quick brush of highlighter across the apples of your cheeks.

3. A quick stroke of tinted lip balm finishes the look.

CHAPTER 5
EYE-CATCHING EYES

It's been said the eyes are the windows to the soul. Wearing eye makeup is like picking out the right curtains. It dresses up your face and can be a fun way to express yourself and feel great.

EYELINER OPTIONS

Eyeliner can be used to highlight the shape of your eyes. Different types can offer a different look. Powder eyeliners give a soft, gentle look. Pencil eyeliners are easy to use and give a stronger outline to the eyes. Liquid eyeliner is the boldest of all and gives a fluid, sleek look.

IF YOU DON'T HAVE POWDER EYELINER but want to try a subtle look, try using a damp cotton swab and a dark eye shadow. Plum, brown, gray, or dark green are great colors for this. Just dab the cotton swab to the color, and apply a very thin line at the base of your top eyelashes. Smudge it for a smokier look.

IF YOU DON'T HAVE A LIQUID LINER, but you're feeling bold, try this trick. Hold a pencil eyeliner under the heat from your hairdryer for a few seconds until it warms up. Test out the warm pencil eyeliner on the back of your hand before you try it on your eyes to get a feel for the new, soft texture. Then lightly run the pencil along the base of your upper lashes to get a smooth, fluid line. Liquid liner can look harsh on the lower lid, so it's probably best to avoid applying it there.

FANTASTIC LASHES

Your eyelashes frame your eyes and draw attention to your inner sparkle. If you ever want to emphasize them, try a little mascara. **Mascaras come in many colors.**

BLACK
If you have dark hair, black mascara might be your best bet.

BROWN
Brown mascara tends to look more natural on people with light brown or blonde hair.

DARK GREEN
Dark green mascara makes hazel eyes shine.

BLUE
Blue mascara is a great way to add drama to your look. It also highlights gray and brown eyes.

PURPLE
Purple mascara can make green or brown eyes pop.

EYE HEALTH

Did you know makeup products have expiration dates? These are important to know, especially for products you use around your eyes. Expired eye makeup can introduce bacteria into your eyes. This could lead to infections that, in rare cases, may damage your vision. Here are general guidelines for how long eye makeup typically lasts.

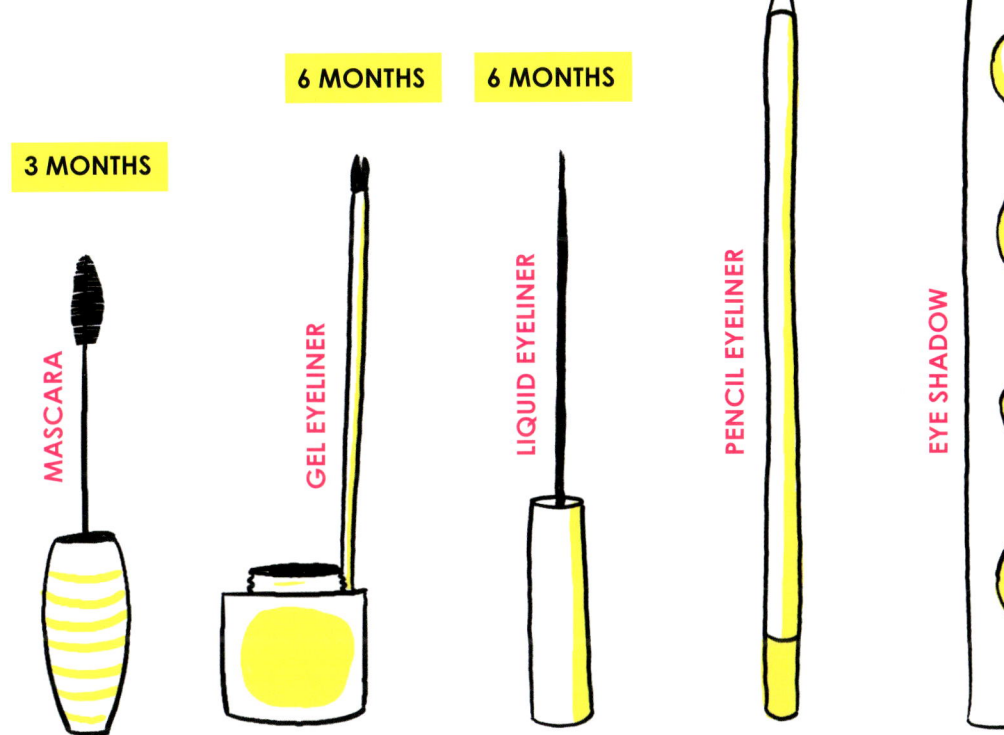

3 MONTHS — MASCARA
6 MONTHS — GEL EYELINER
6 MONTHS — LIQUID EYELINER
1 YEAR — PENCIL EYELINER
1 YEAR — EYE SHADOW

If your mascara starts to dry out before its expiration date, don't fret! There's an easy way to make it last a little longer. Just add a drop or two of saline solution to the bottle. Then insert the wand and stir or shake to mix. Don't pump the wand in and out of the tube. This just lets in more air, which dries out the mascara even more.

TIP
Looking for saline? If you wear contact lenses, your storing solution is probably made from saline.

You draw attention to your lips every time you speak. Finding the perfect lip shade lets you express yourself without saying a word.

CHAPTER 6

LIP HACKS TO LOVE

LET'S BE CLEAR

Clear lip gloss is a makeup marvel. It adds shine to your lips for the perfect pout. It also moisturizes and protects the delicate skin of your lips. But that's not all. Clear lip gloss can get you out of all kinds of binds.

- Spread a little clear lip gloss on a sticky or jammed zipper to free up the tangled teeth.
- Use clear lip gloss to tame flyaway hairs from your ponytail.
- Rub clear lip gloss on your finger to help slip off a ring that just won't budge.
- Control crazy eyebrow hairs with a dab of clear gloss.
- Apply clear lip gloss to super dry, scaly skin for relief.

DON'T TOSS IT!

It can feel tragic when a favorite makeup item breaks before its expiration date. But getting crafty and creative will help you make the most of crushed cosmetics.

- **Crumbled eye shadow** can make a bold and beautiful lip color. Simply mix the powdered shadow with some Vaseline and store it in a resealable container.

- **Broken or melted lipstick** doesn't have to end up in the trash. Scoop it out and press it into an empty contact lens case. Then simply apply it with your finger.

MAKE YOUR SMILE SMOOTH

Lip colors come in a rainbow of colors and shades. Some are shimmery. Others are matte. Some add just a little color, while others are more pigmented. No matter which style you choose, lip color is a fun way to emphasize your lovely lips.

Matte lip colors have no shine at all. They look flat and smooth. To get the smoothest matte lip color possible, here's a hack for you.

WHAT YOU NEED:

matte lipstick + clean mascara wand +

gentle facial cleanser + washcloth

WHAT TO DO:

Gently rub your lips with the clean mascara wand. You will see that small bits of dead skin are gently being brushed off. Use the washcloth to wash your lips with the gentle facial cleanser. Dry them thoroughly and immediately apply lip balm so that your lips don't dry out. Then add the matte lipstick to your smooth, beautiful lips.

Addicted to LIP BALM?

Do you feel like you can't leave home without your lip balm? Don't schedule that lip balm intervention quite yet. A common cosmetic myth tells us that lip balm is addictive. This urban legend claims that lip balms contain ingredients that actually dry out your lips, making you want to reapply. As scandalous as this sounds, it's not true. The skin on your lips is simply prone to drying out on its own. Lip balm is actually very helpful.

MAKEUP BRUSH HACKS

If you've ever seen a makeup artist at a salon or department store, you've probably noticed his or her arsenal of brushes. There are makeup brushes for nearly every type of makeup — foundation brushes, blush brushes, eye shadow brushes, and even lipstick brushes. Different types of brushes make it easier to apply different types of makeup with better control.

Most people don't have a giant selection of makeup brushes at their disposal. But you can still get the look you want without a specific type of brush. Try these hacks to get a professional look with no makeup brushes at all.

INSTEAD OF AN EYEBROW BRUSH: ▶▶▶▶▶▶ USE A CLEAN TOOTHBRUSH.

Use it to smooth and direct your brows.

INSTEAD OF AN EYE SHADOW BRUSH: ▶▶▶▶▶ DIP A COTTON SWAB IN EYE SHADOW.

Gently brush it across your lids.

INSTEAD OF A BLUSH BRUSH: ▶▶▶▶▶▶▶▶ USE A COTTON BALL OR TISSUE.

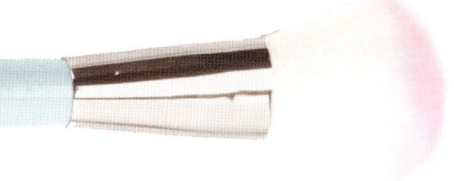

Dip the tissue or cotton ball into your blush and gently sweep it across the apples of your cheeks.

INSTEAD OF A FOUNDATION BRUSH: ▶▶▶▶▶ USE YOUR FINGERS.

Your middle and ring fingers are probably the softest while offering the most control. First, wash your hands. Next, dab foundation under your eyes, around your nose, and on your forehead. Gently work the foundation outward to cover your whole face.

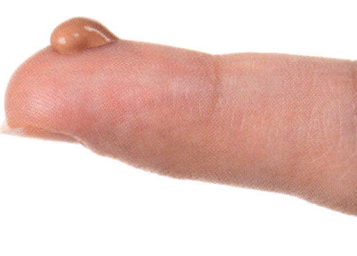

CHAPTER 7
KEEP IT CLEAN

Did you know you're supposed to wash your makeup brushes? Over time, they collect old makeup, dirt, bacteria, and dead skin cells. You should wash them every two weeks to keep them from getting downright dirty. Washing your brushes can lengthen their shelf life and help keep your skin clear and healthy.

BATHING BRUSHES

WHAT YOU NEED:

| used makeup brushes | baby shampoo | paper towels | small bowl of warm water | washcloth |

 +  +  +  +

WHAT TO DO:

Step 1
Wipe brush bristles against a dry paper towel to remove as much excess makeup as possible.

Step 2
Add a few drops of baby shampoo to a small bowl of warm water.

Step 3
Swish brush bristles around in the soapy water. Try not to get the handle of the brush wet. This could loosen the glue holding the bristles in place.

Step 4
Hold the bristles under the faucet to rinse away any excess soap.

Step 5
Dry the bristles as much as possible with the dry washcloth.

Step 6
Smooth the bristles out into the original shape and let dry on a paper towel.

SQUEAKY CLEAN
CLEANSER HACKS

Makeup can clog your pores and lead to blemishes. It's important to clean it all off each night before you go to bed. Makeup removers are special types of cleansers designed to help clean away cosmetics.

FACE-SAVING TIPS

Tip #1 You may need to use a stronger cleanser in the summer. Summer skin tends to be oilier than winter skin.

Tip #2 Don't just splash your face and go. Massage your cleanser in. A couple of minutes should do the trick.

Tip #3 Rub your skin gently. Scrubbing too hard can irritate the delicate skin of your face.

Tip #4 Rinse your face with lukewarm water. Cold water won't rinse off all the residue, but hot water can irritate your skin.

SURPRISE SUBSTITUTES

If you don't have a special makeup remover, you can probably find a substitute right in your house. Try these hacks to remove your makeup, and let your skin breathe and your natural beauty shine.

▶ AVOCADO

Swipe a clean cotton swab along the inside of a fresh avocado to collect some of the oil. Then use the cotton swab to gently rub off pesky makeup. Wash the oil off with a cleanser when your makeup is all removed.

▶ BABY SHAMPOO

This gentle cleanser is a great go-to for makeup removal in a pinch, and it's gentle enough for even the most sensitive skin.

▶ PETROLEUM JELLY

This is a great tool for removing extra stubborn makeup, such as mascara, once you've already washed your face. Get the last bit of makeup off with a small smear of petroleum jelly.

▶ UNSCENTED LOTION

Dip a cotton ball or tissue into a small amount of unscented lotion for a gentle, effective makeup remover. Wash your face with a gentle cleanser when you're done.

Awesome girls are smart, strong, and ready for anything. Be sure you're prepped for adventure with a bag packed with essentials. These products will make you feel confident, no matter what the day brings.

CHAPTER 8
YOUR ON-THE-GO ESSENTIALS

BASIC NECESSITIES

Put the following items in a resealable plastic baggie. Then transfer this baggie from your purse to your school bag.

Mascara
A quick swipe of mascara will instantly wake up your face if you're feeling less energetic than usual.

Blush
Use a little blush on your cheeks, or apply it to your lips and eyes for a healthy glow.

Unscented lotion
Moisturize your skin, remove unruly makeup, or mix with foundation for a light base color.

Clear lip gloss or lip balm
Freshen your lips, moisturize skin, tame wild hairs, or unstick a zipper.

Sunscreen
Keep your skin safe from the sun year-round. Even in the winter, exposed skin can suffer from sun damage.

Tissues
Tissues can come in handy if you need to tame bleeding eyeliner or lipstick, and, obviously, to wipe your nose.

Deodorant
Keep this on hand in case you find yourself in a hot or stressful situation. You never know when break-through perspiration will rear its ugly head.

The most essential thing you'll need to face the day isn't part of a makeup or skincare routine. It's confidence. Be yourself. There's no one in the world quite like you. Keep this in mind as you head out for school, sports, or a day with friends. Remember that you are unique, important, and strong. Let your makeup highlight who you are, not cover it up.

CHAPTER 9
BE YOUR BEST SELF

BRIGHTEN YOUR DAY!

Sometimes it can be hard to feel confident. Try this activity to make sure every morning is a reminder of how incredible you really are.

WHAT YOU NEED:

markers, pens, and colored pencils   note cards   tape

WHAT TO DO:

Step 1 Think of a saying that provides you with support and encouragement. You might choose a sentence such as, "I am beautiful," or "I am amazing." Try to brainstorm something that will make you feel confident and powerful when you see it.

Step 2 Write your affirmation on a note card in a bright, exciting color. Decorate the card in a way that inspires you.

Step 3 Tape your card somewhere you will see it every morning — perhaps on your makeup mirror.

Step 4 Read your affirmation every day. It should remind you daily that true beauty comes from the inside out.

READ MORE

Shoket, Ann. Seventeen *Ultimate Guide to Beauty*. Philadelphia: Running Press, 2012.

Traig, Jennifer. *Makeup: Things to Make and Do.* Crafty Girl. San Francisco: Chronicle, 2013.

Trew, Sally. *Idiots Guides: Making Natural Beauty Products.* New York City: Penguin Group, 2013.

ABOUT THE AUTHOR

Rebecca Rissman is a nonfiction author and editor. She has written more than 300 books about history, science, and art. Her book *Shapes in Sports* earned a starred review from *Booklist,* and her series Animal Spikes and Spines received *Learning Magazine*'s 2013 Teachers Choice for Children's Books. Rissman especially enjoys writing about fashion. She studied fashion history as part of her master's degree in English Literature at Loyola University Chicago. She lives in Chicago, Illinois, with her husband and two daughters.